OCR

A LEVEL YEAR 2

WORKBOOK

FOR THE 2015 SPECIFICATIONS

Economics
Macroeconomics 2

Terry Cook

Contents

WORKBOOK

Topic 1 Economic policy objectives and indicators of macroeconomic performance 3
    Economic growth and development 3
    Unemployment/employment 8
    Inflation 10
    Income distribution and welfare 10
    Trends in macroeconomic indicators 12

Topic 2 Aggregate demand and aggregate supply 17
    Aggregate demand 17
    Aggregate supply 18
    Macroeconomic equilibrium 19
    The Phillips curve 19
    The economic cycle 21

Topic 3 The application of policy instruments 25
    Fiscal policy 25
    Monetary policy 27

Topic 4 The global context 31
    Globalisation 31
    International trade 32
    Exchange rates 33
    Trade policies and negotiations 34

Topic 5 The financial sector 40
    The role of the financial sector in the real economy 40
    The financial sector in developing and emerging economies 43
    The role of the central bank 44
    Financial regulation 45

① This workbook will prepare you for OCR A-level Unit H460/02 Macroeconomics.

② The workbook focuses on these areas of study:
- economic policy objectives and indicators of macroeconomic performance
- aggregate demand and aggregate supply
- the application of policy instruments
- the global context
- the financial sector

③ The examination is 2 hours long and you will need to answer a range of questions, some requiring relatively short answers and others requiring longer answers which need to be planned in the same way as essays. Some of these questions will carry only 2 or 4 marks, but some will carry as many as 25 marks.

For each topic you will find:
- stimulus material
- short-answer questions that build up to exam-style questions
- spaces for you to write or plan your answers
- questions which test your mathematical skills

④

⑤ Answering the questions will help you to build your skills and meet the four assessment objectives AO1 (knowledge and understanding), AO2 (application), AO3 (analysis) and AO4 (evaluation).

⑥ You still need to read your textbook and refer to your revision guides and lesson notes.

⑦ Marks available are indicated for all questions so that you can gauge the level of detail required in your answers.

⑧ Timings are given for the exam-style questions to make your practice as realistic as possible.

⑨ Answers are available at www.hoddereducation.co.uk/workbookanswers.

Topic 1

Economic policy objectives and indicators of macroeconomic performance

Economic growth and development

The structure of an economy

It is possible to explain the structure of an economy in terms of primary, secondary and tertiary sectors.

The primary sector refers to that part of the economy which includes extractive industries, such as agriculture, forestry, fishing, mining and quarrying. The secondary sector refers to that part of the economy which includes manufacturing and construction, such as a car producing factory and the building of a motorway. The tertiary sector refers to that part of the economy which includes services, such as transportation and education.

> **1** Explain what is meant by the primary, secondary and tertiary sectors of an economy. (AO2)
>
> **4 marks**

Economic development

Economic growth was discussed in the Macroeconomics 1 workbook. This Macroeconomics 2 workbook goes beyond economic growth to consider economic development. Although there is a clear relationship between economic growth and economic development, they also need to be clearly distinguished.

Economic growth refers to an increase in real output over a period of time, usually measured through changes in real, as opposed to nominal, gross domestic product (GDP).

Economic development is a broader concept that takes into account more than just the material standard of living in a country. For example, it could also include life expectancy and education. The human development index (HDI) goes beyond GDP per head. There is now an even broader measure of economic development, called the multidimensional poverty index (MPI).

Economic development refers to the process by which a country may experience a reallocation of resources away from the primary sector towards the secondary and tertiary sectors. It involves a country moving away from being a developing country and towards being a developed country. The economist W. W. Rostow has identified five stages in the process of development. These are the traditional society, the transitional stage, the take-off, the drive to maturity and the stage of high mass consumption.

2 Distinguish between the human development index (HDI) and the multidimensional poverty index (MPI). (AO1) — 2 marks

3 Distinguish between economic growth and economic development. (AO1) — 2 marks

4 Explain what is meant by economic development. (AO2) — 4 marks

Sustainable development

Sustainability refers to the need of the present generation to take into account the potential effects of decisions taken today on future generations. The needs of future generations should not be compromised as a result of meeting the needs of the present generation. For example, a greater emphasis should be placed on renewable, in contrast to non-renewable, resources. A reduction of CO_2 emissions would be another way of bringing about sustainable development in a country.

One of the clearest definitions of sustainability came from the World Commission on Environment and Development in 1987: 'Sustainable development is development that meets the needs of the present without compromising the ability of future generations to meet their own needs.'

The World Bank, in 1994, stated that economic growth 'brings with it the risk of appalling environmental damage. Alternatively, it could bring with it better environmental protection, cleaner air and water, and the virtual elimination of acute poverty. Policy choices will make the difference.'

5 Explain what is meant by sustainable development. (AO2) 4 marks

Aid and trade

Economic growth and development can be promoted through aid and trade.

Overseas or official development assistance (ODA) is a term used by the Development Assistance Committee (DAC) of the Organisation for Economic Co-operation and Development (OECD) to measure aid given to various countries to promote economic development.

Economic development can also be promoted through trade. If a country is able to export its products to more countries, this should encourage economic and social development, such as through the employment of a greater number of workers.

6 Distinguish between aid and trade as ways of promoting economic growth and development. (AO1) 2 marks

7 Explain how overseas development assistance (ODA) and trade can promote economic growth and development. (AO2) 4 marks

Indicators

There are a number of possible indicators that can be used to measure economic growth and economic development. These include:
- gross domestic product (GDP) per head or per capita
- the human development index (HDI)
- the multidimensional poverty index (MPI)
- the genuine progress indicator (GPI)
- the Easterlin paradox
- the Office for National Statistics (ONS) Measuring National Well-being programme

8 Evaluate the usefulness of the various indicators to measure economic growth and development. (AO4)   *12 marks*

The role of international organisations in promoting economic growth and development

There are three particularly important international financial institutions: the International Monetary Fund (IMF), the World Bank and the World Trade Organization (WTO).

The International Monetary Fund (IMF)

The IMF was established in 1944. Its website states: 'The IMF promotes international monetary cooperation and exchange rate stability, facilitates the balanced growth of international trade, and provides resources to help members in balance of payments difficulties or to assist with poverty reduction.' It now has 189 member countries. A more stable world monetary system is likely to promote economic growth and development by providing support to those countries in financial difficulties.

9 Describe the purpose of the International Monetary Fund. (AO1) *2 marks*

10 Explain the role of the International Monetary Fund in promoting economic growth and development. (AO2) *4 marks*

The World Bank

The World Bank was also established in 1944. It is made up of five organisations: the International Bank for Reconstruction and Development (IBRD), the International Development Association (IDA), the International Finance Corporation (IFC), the Multilateral Investment Guarantee Agency (MIGA) and the International Centre for Settlement of Investment Disputes (ICSID). Through the provision of loans, the World Bank is able to promote economic growth and development.

11 Describe the purpose of the World Bank. (AO1) *2 marks*

12 Explain the role of the World Bank in promoting economic growth and development. (AO2) *4 marks*

The World Trade Organization (WTO)

The WTO was established in 1995. Its website states: 'The World Trade Organization deals with the global rules of trade between nations. Its main function is to ensure that trade flows as smoothly, predictably and freely as possible.' The WTO now has 163 member countries. It is involved in a series of discussions to achieve its objectives. The current round of trade negotiations is called the Doha Round and its aim is to achieve major reform of the international trading system through the introduction of lower trade barriers and revised trade rules. These discussions have been taking place since 2001.

13 Describe the purpose of the World Trade Organization. (AO1) — *2 marks*

14 Explain the role of the World Trade Organization in promoting economic growth and development. (AO2) — *4 marks*

Unemployment/employment

The Macroeconomics 1 workbook covered a number of aspects of employment and unemployment. In addition to those, you need to understand the natural or non-accelerating inflation rate of unemployment and the causes and consequences of changes in the pattern of employment.

The natural/non-accelerating inflation rate of unemployment (NAIRU)

The natural rate of unemployment is also known as NAIRU. This refers to the level of unemployment at which the rate of inflation is stable and constant. It is the level of unemployment in an economy that cannot be reduced in the long term by increasing aggregate demand. It is often associated with Monetarist economists, such as Milton Friedman.

15 State what is meant by NAIRU. (AO1) — *2 marks*

Once unemployment falls below a certain level, the rate of inflation is likely to accelerate. Once unemployment rises above a certain level, the rate of inflation is likely to fall. Figure 1 shows this relationship. This level of unemployment therefore occurs when an economy is at full employment, i.e. when the labour market is in equilibrium.

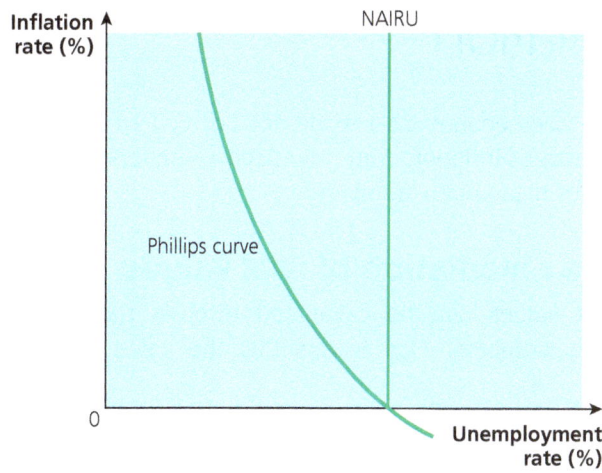

Figure 1 The non-accelerating inflation rate of unemployment

16 Explain what is meant by the non-accelerating inflation rate of unemployment. (AO2) 4 marks

The causes and consequences of changes in the pattern of employment

Patterns of employment and unemployment can have a number of consequences for an economy. These can include technological unemployment and cyclical unemployment. In terms of employment, there has been a steady increase in the UK and there are more workers employed than ever before.

17 Analyse the causes and consequences of changes in the pattern of employment. (AO3) 8 marks

Inflation

The Macroeconomics 1 workbook covered a number of aspects of inflation. You now need to understand real values using index numbers.

The calculation of real values

Real values can be calculated through the use of index numbers. This means that the value will use a base year, usually expressed as 100. The effect is that the use of constant prices will give a value in relation to the purchasing power of a nominal sum of money. This can be seen in terms of real income or real output.

Consumer prices index and retail prices index

An index is used to measure the rate of inflation in an economy. In the UK the two main indices that are used for this purpose are the consumer prices index (CPI) and the retail prices index (RPI).

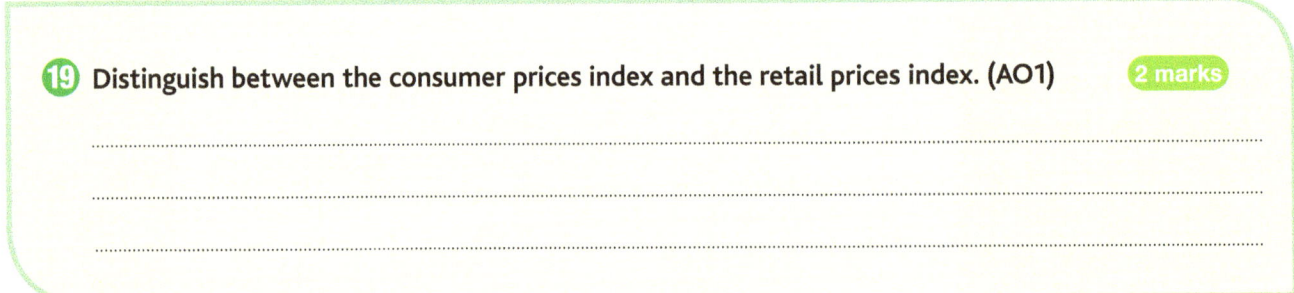

Income distribution and welfare

The Lorenz curve

A Lorenz curve can be used to explain how income and wealth are distributed in an economy.

A Lorenz curve is a graphical representation showing inequality in the distribution of income and wealth in an economy. An example of one can be seen in Figure 2.

The 45-degree (45°) line shows the situation if a certain percentage of the population received the same percentage of income, i.e. it is the line of equality. The Lorenz curve shows the extent to which the equality of income deviates from this 45-degree line. The more unequal the distribution of income, the more the Lorenz curve will deviate from the 45-degree line. Conversely, the more equal the distribution of income, the closer the Lorenz curve will be to the 45-degree line.

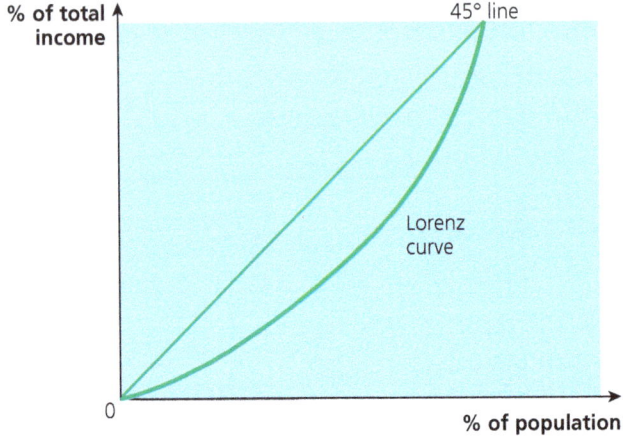

Figure 2 The Lorenz curve

20 Explain how a Lorenz curve can help in the explanation of the distribution of income and wealth in an economy. (AO2) *4 marks*

The Gini coefficient

Figure 2 illustrates the Lorenz curve, a visual representation of the degree of equality/inequality in the distribution of income and wealth in a particular economy.

The Gini coefficient is the ratio of the area between the line of equality and the Lorenz curve and the total area under the line of equality.

If there was absolute equality in the distribution of income and wealth in an economy, the Gini coefficient would be equal to 0. If there was absolute inequality in this distribution, the Gini coefficient would be equal to 1.

Table 1 shows the Gini coefficient of a number of countries.

Country	Gini coefficient
Sweden	0.259
Switzerland	0.303
New Zealand	0.330
UK	0.345
USA	0.378
Chile	0.394
Turkey	0.409
Mexico	0.476

Table 1 The Gini coefficient

21 Describe the Gini coefficient. (AO1) *2 marks*

22 Explain the usefulness of the Gini coefficient in terms of Table 1. (AO2) *(4 marks)*

Absolute poverty and relative poverty

It is possible to distinguish between two different types of poverty.

Absolute poverty is where people are unable to afford the basic necessities of life. For example, this is where certain people are malnourished and homeless. In 1990, the World Bank stated that absolute poverty existed when people were trying to survive on less than US$1.00 a day. In 2005, this figure was revised to US$1.25.

Relative poverty is where some people have less income than others in a society and are therefore unable to buy what these others are able to afford. Relative poverty is defined in terms of the context of a particular society. This situation does not necessarily mean that the people in relative poverty are poor in absolute terms.

23 Distinguish between absolute and relative poverty. (AO2) *(4 marks)*

Trends in macroeconomic indicators

The key trends in UK macroeconomic performance in the last 20 years can be explained through:

- economic growth
- inflation
- employment/unemployment
- the balance of payments

24 Explain the key trends in UK macroeconomic performance in the last 20 years. (AO2) *(4 marks)*

Exam-style questions

25 Evaluate the relationship between economic growth, changes in the structure of an economy, economic development and sustainable development. (AO4) — 25 marks

26 Analyse why the HDI is considered to be a better measure of economic development than GDP per capita. (AO3) [12 marks]

27 a A person's income has increased by 5.2%. The rate of inflation is 2.9%. Calculate the increase in the person's real income. (AO1) — 2 marks

b Explain why economists are interested in changes in real, as opposed to nominal, income. (AO2) — 4 marks

For multiple-choice questions, circle the letter of the answer that you think is correct.

28 Which of the following occupations is in the primary sector of an economy? (AO1) — 1 mark

A Builder

B Factory worker

C Farmer

D Teacher

29 According to Rostow, which was the third stage in the process of development? (AO1) — 1 mark

A The drive to maturity

B The stage of high mass consumption

C The take-off

D The transitional stage

30 Which of the following indicators includes the quality of water? (AO1) — 1 mark

A Gross domestic product per capita

B The Easterlin paradox

C The human development index

D The multidimensional poverty index

31 If the distribution of income in an economy was absolutely equal, the Gini coefficient would be equal to: (AO1) — 1 mark

A 0.000

B 0.333

C 0.500

D 1.000

32 Which of the following figures gives an indication of absolute poverty? Living on less than: (AO1) *1 mark*

    A US$0.50 a day

    B US$1.25 a day

    C US$3.00 a day

    D US$5.00 a day

33 The HDI (human development index) now measures standard of living through: (AO1) *1 mark*

    A gross domestic income per capita

    B gross national income per capita

    C gross national product per capita

    D net national product per capita

34 The idea that the average level of happiness does not vary greatly with national income per person is known as the: (AO1) *1 mark*

    A Bretton Woods paradox

    B Easterlin paradox

    C Nairu paradox

    D Todaro paradox

35 Which of the following Gini coefficients would show the situation where there was absolute equality in the distribution of income and wealth in an economy? (AO1) *1 mark*

    A 0.00

    B 0.25

    C 0.75

    D 1.00

36 Which of the following can be used to show how income and wealth are distributed in an economy? (AO1) *1 mark*

    A Easterlin curve

    B Gini curve

    C Lorenz curve

    D MPI curve

Topic 2

Aggregate demand and aggregate supply

Aggregate demand

The accelerator

The accelerator can be used to explain the relationship between investment and the rate of change of output. The key aspect of the accelerator is that it is not the *level* of output that determines investment but the *rate of change* of that output. Investment is therefore a function of a change in national income.

If the level of output grows faster than it did before, the rate at which new productive capacity is created will need to increase. On the other hand, if the level of output stabilises, it will not be necessary to have any additional investment, other than what is needed to take account of the depreciation of existing machines. In this situation, investment will actually fall.

The accelerator therefore explains why investment fluctuates more than output. It relates to the induced effect on investment of a change in national income and it assumes a fixed capital–output ratio.

1 Define the term 'accelerator'. (AO1) — 2 marks

2 Explain how the accelerator can be used to account for the level of investment in an economy. (AO2) — 4 marks

Aggregate supply

The Keynesian and neo-classical approaches to aggregate supply

It is possible to distinguish between two different approaches to aggregate supply.

The Keynesian approach to aggregate supply is that the AS curve is a horizontal, perfectly elastic, line up to the full employment level of real output (Figure 3). An increase in aggregate demand, such as from AD to AD_1, will increase the level of real output but not the level of prices. When the full employment level of real output is reached, however, the level of prices will increase so that the AS curve now becomes a vertical, perfectly inelastic, line.

The neo-classical approach to aggregate supply is that the AS curve is a vertical line (Figure 4). Any increase in aggregate demand, such as from AD to AD_1, will increase the price level, but not output and employment. In order to increase output and employment, supply-side policies are needed to shift the AS curve to the right.

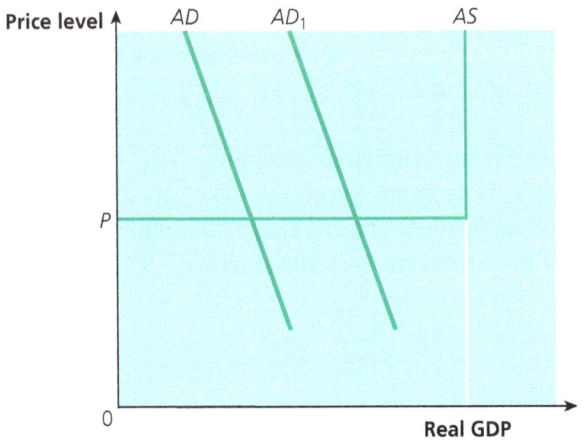

Figure 3 The Keynesian approach to aggregate supply

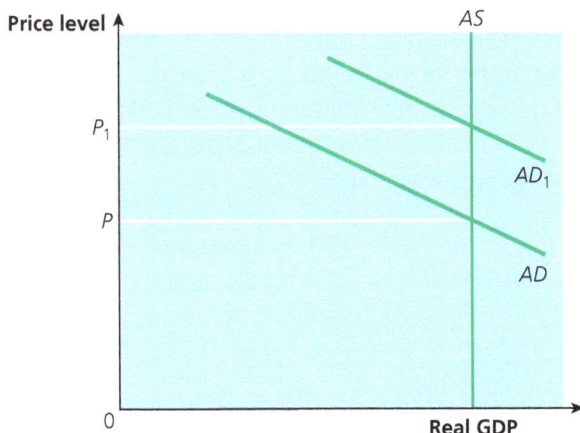

Figure 4 The neo-classical approach to aggregate supply

3 Distinguish between the Keynesian and neo-classical approaches to aggregate supply. (AO2)

4 marks

Macroeconomic equilibrium

There are different schools of thought on how the macroeconomy operates. These include the Keynesian, the neo-classical and the Austrian schools of thought.

> **4** Explain the differences between the Keynesian, the neo-classical and the Austrian schools of thought on how the macroeconomy operates. (AO2)   *4 marks*

The Phillips curve

The Phillips curve can be seen in Figure 1 in the section on the non-accelerating inflation rate of unemployment (NAIRU).

It shows the relationship between the rate of inflation and the rate of unemployment in an economy, emphasising the trade-off between them. Thus, the Phillips curve is downward sloping, as shown in Figure 5.

However, it is also possible to consider the expectations-augmented Phillips curve. If people have strong expectations of inflation, they are likely to want to negotiate large wage increases to ensure that there is no loss in the purchasing power of the money they earn. The effect of this is that at any given level of unemployment, the rate of inflation will increase. It therefore becomes necessary to distinguish between the short-run and the long-run Phillips curve (Figure 6).

In the short run, the Phillips curve moves upwards, i.e. it shifts to the right, and so the trade-off between inflation and unemployment remains, but now at a higher rate of inflation than was previously the case. The Phillips curve may therefore become vertical in the long run.

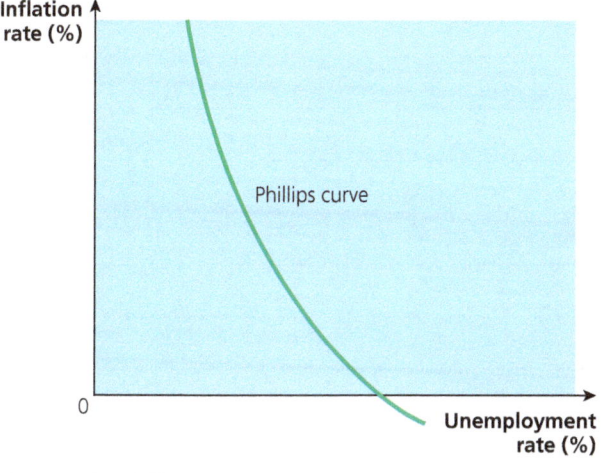

Figure 5 The Phillips curve

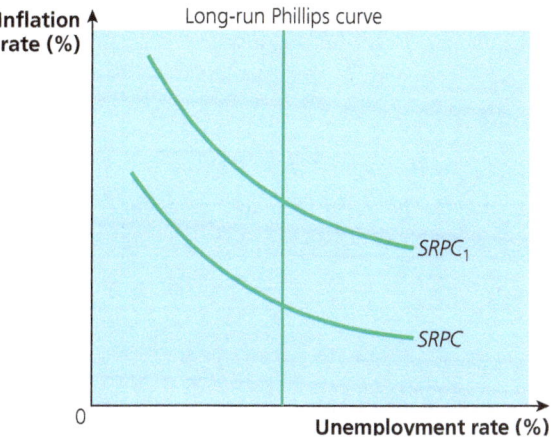

Figure 6 The expectations-augmented Phillips curve

5 Distinguish between the short-run and the long-run Phillips curve. (AO1) 2 marks

Workers continue to have strong expectations of inflation and this is known as the adaptive-expectations hypothesis, i.e. they base their view of future inflation rates on what has happened in the past. The short-run trade-off comes about because of 'money illusion', i.e. workers focus on money wages and not real wages.

In the long run, there is no trade-off between the rate of inflation and the rate of unemployment and the economy returns to its long-run equilibrium. The real wage is restored to long-run equilibrium and the economy is at full employment.

6 Analyse why the Phillips curve is vertical in the long run. (AO3) 8 marks

The economic cycle

The different stages of the economic cycle

The long-run trend rate of economic growth will be influenced by the different stages of the trade cycle. This is also known as the business cycle or the economic cycle.

These different stages of the trade, business or economic cycle are shown in Figure 7.

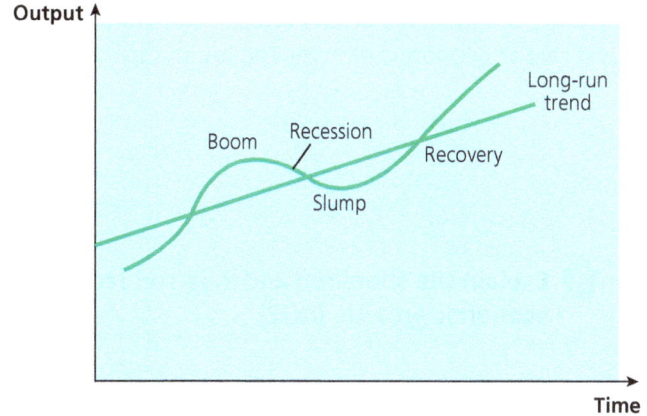

Figure 7 The trade, business or economic cycle

7 Identify the four stages of the economic cycle. (AO1) *2 marks*

8 Explain the different stages of the economic cycle. (AO2) *4 marks*

Actual and trend rates of growth

The long-run trend of economic growth is generally shown as a straight line in a diagram, but an economy is most likely to be at a point above or below this straight line and only occasionally actually on the line. It is possible to see whether the long-run trend of economic growth deviates from what would generally be expected of it.

The factors which determine the trend rate of economic growth

There are a number of factors which can determine the trend rate of economic growth. These can include:

- changes in aggregate demand
- changes in aggregate supply
- the interaction of the multiplier and the accelerator
- the economic cycle
- the quantity and quality of the labour force
- the capital stock

9 Explain the short-run and long-run factors which determine the trend rate of economic growth. (AO2) **4 marks**

10 Analyse the importance of the interaction of the multiplier and the accelerator. (AO3) **8 marks**

Output gaps

An output gap shows the difference between the actual output and the potential output of an economy when it is working at full capacity. It is possible to look at changes in real GDP over a period of time and compare this with the long-run trend rate of growth to see if there is a deviation or divergence. This output gap can be either positive or negative.

Figure 8 shows both a negative and a positive output gap. Points *A* and *D* are on the long-run trend line, but points *B* and *C* are below this trend line. Between *A* and *D*, below the long-run trend line, there is a negative output gap.

Beyond point *D*, the actual GDP line is above the long-run trend line, e.g. at points *E* and *F*. Between points *D* and *G*, above the long-run trend line, there is a positive output gap.

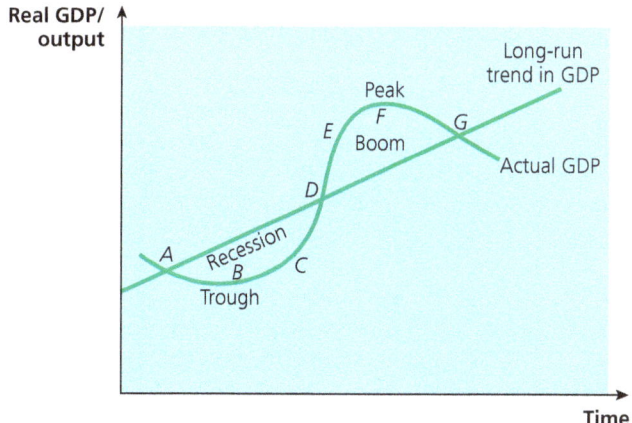

Figure 8 The output gap

11 State what is meant by an output gap. (AO1) *2 marks*

....
....
....
....

12 Distinguish between a positive and a negative output gap. (AO1) *2 marks*

....
....
....
....
....

Exam-style questions

13 a Calculate the size of the national income multiplier from the following information. An economy has a marginal propensity to save of 0.1, a marginal propensity to tax of 0.3 and a marginal propensity to import of 0.4. (AO1) *12* *2 marks*

....
....
....
....

b Explain the factors which determine the size of the national income multiplier. (AO2) `6 marks`

For multiple-choice questions, circle the letter of the answer that you think is correct.

14 The accelerator shows the relationship between change in investment and: (AO1) `1 mark`

    A the change in the level of prices

    B the change of output

    C the rate of change of output

    D the rate of change of unemployment

15 The Phillips curve shows the trade-off between: (AO1) `1 mark`

    A the rate of inflation and the rate of economic growth

    B the rate of inflation and the rate of unemployment

    C the rate of investment and the rate of unemployment

    D the rate of unemployment and the balance of payments

16 Economic growth is at its most rapid at which stage of the economic cycle? (AO1) `1 mark`

    A Boom

    B Recession

    C Recovery

    D Slump

17 An output gap shows the difference between actual output and the potential output of an economy when: (AO1) `1 mark`

    A it is working at full capacity

    B the marginal propensity to tax increases

    C the savings ratio falls

    D there is some spare capacity

Topic 3

The application of policy instruments

Fiscal policy

Average and marginal tax rates

It is important to be able to distinguish between average and marginal tax rates. The average tax rate is the average percentage of total income which is paid in taxes. The marginal tax rate is the percentage of additional income which is paid in taxes. If a tax system is progressive, the average rate of tax will be lower than the marginal rate of tax.

> **1** Distinguish between average and marginal tax rates. (AO1)   **2 marks**

The Laffer curve

The Laffer curve shows the relationship between the rate of tax and the revenue that is obtained from it. The curve shows that higher tax rates will eventually lead to a decline in the revenue received from a tax, i.e. they act as a disincentive for firms, in relation to corporation tax, and for employees, in relation to income tax. Although the rate of tax is higher, fewer people are actually working and so the revenue obtained from the tax will be lower. In such a situation, a tax cut could lead to an increase in revenue for a government because more people will want to work and firms will want to expand.

The Laffer curve (Figure 9) shows that at relatively low levels of taxation, the revenue from tax will increase if the tax rates are raised. On the other hand, at relatively high rates of taxation, the revenue from tax will reduce if the tax rates are raised, demonstrating the disincentive effect of a tax increase.

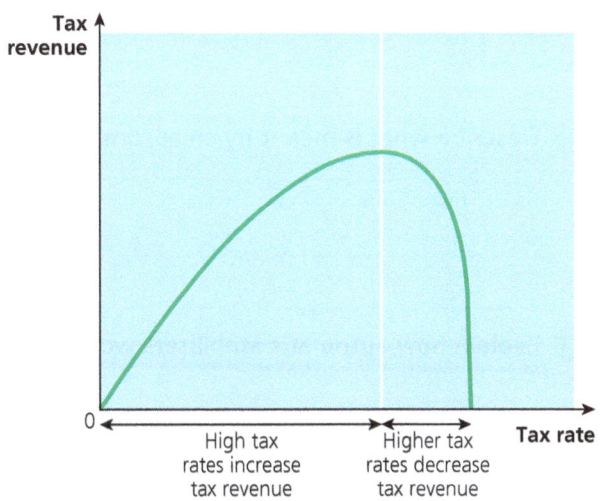

Figure 9 The Laffer curve

2 Explain how the Laffer curve can demonstrate the disincentive effect of an increase in tax. (AO2) `4 marks`

Automatic stabilisers

An automatic stabiliser is a fiscal policy which works to reduce fluctuations in income over the course of the trade cycle without needing any further adjustment.

Government spending on unemployment benefits, for example, can be regarded as an automatic stabiliser. During a recession, government spending will automatically rise when the level of unemployment increases. This extra spending will compensate for the reduction in the earned income of workers. The effect of this is that although consumption is still likely to fall, it will fall less slowly than would have been the case if there were no benefits and the unemployed received no income once they had become unemployed.

Income tax can also be regarded as an automatic stabiliser. As incomes rise in the boom phase of the trade cycle, the revenue gained from income tax will rise more than proportionately because income tax is a progressive tax. As incomes fall in the recession phase of the trade cycle, the revenue gained from income tax will fall more than proportionately. The effect of income tax working as an automatic stabiliser in this way is that income tax takes more spending power out of an economy during a boom than it does in a recession. This helps to counteract the fluctuations in aggregate demand and so reduce the impact of these cyclical events.

3 Describe what is meant by an automatic stabiliser. (AO1) `2 marks`

4 Explain how automatic stabilisers work to achieve economic stability. (AO2) `4 marks`

Crowding in and crowding out

Fiscal policy can lead to a situation of 'crowding out' when it is expansionary. If there is an increase in government spending and/or a decrease in tax revenue, increased borrowing may be necessary to finance this deficit. If a government needs to borrow more money to finance its increased expenditure, this could reduce investment spending by the private sector, i.e. the increased borrowing 'crowds out' private investing. Crowding out can thus be seen as a situation where increased public expenditure diverts money or resources away from the private sector.

There can also be a situation of 'crowding in' when there is a budget deficit at a time of an economic recession or depression. If a government decides to increase its spending, this can lead to higher private investment. Deficit spending by a government is likely to stimulate economic activity and, as an economy grows, private firms may be encouraged to expand and so investment will be encouraged, not discouraged as the 'crowding out' hypothesis would suggest.

> **5** Explain how crowding out and crowding in can occur as a result of fiscal policy. (AO2) **4 marks**

Monetary policy

The liquidity trap

The liquidity trap refers to a situation in the liquidity preference theory where an increase in the money supply, beyond a certain point, does not affect the interest rate. Normally, an increase in the money supply will lead to a fall in the interest rate, but when the demand for money curve becomes horizontal, such a shift to the right will have no effect on the interest rate. The interest rate will fall to a point beyond which it cannot go any lower. This is shown in Figure 10.

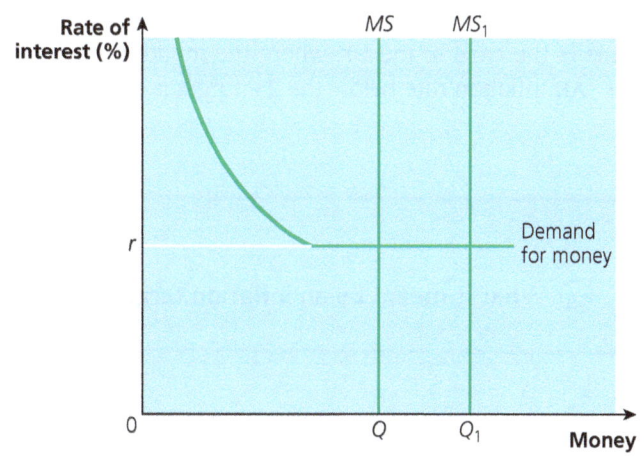

Figure 10 The liquidity trap

6 Explain what is meant by the liquidity trap. (AO2) 4 marks

....
....
....
....
....
....

Symmetric and asymmetric inflation targeting

Symmetric inflation targeting is where a central bank is required to respond to a situation where the rate of inflation in an economy is either too high or too low. This is the case in the UK where the inflation target is 2%. An inflation rate below the 2% target is regarded as a problem, as is an inflation rate above the target. The inflation target is therefore symmetrical.

Non-symmetric, or asymmetric, inflation targeting is when a central bank is required to take action only when the rate of inflation is too high or only when it is too low. Usually this will be when the rate of inflation is too high.

7 What is meant by an inflation target? (AO1) 2 marks

....
....

Exam-style questions

8 Evaluate, using the Laffer curve, the relationship between the tax rate and tax revenue. (AO4)

⏱ 18   **12 marks**

9 Distinguish between symmetric and asymmetric inflation targeting. (AO2) — 4 marks

....

....

....

....

....

....

....

For multiple-choice questions, circle the letter of the answer that you think is correct.

10 If a tax system is progressive, the average rate of tax will be: (AO1) — 1 mark

   A equal to the marginal rate of tax

   B exactly twice as high as the marginal rate of tax

   C higher than the marginal rate of tax

   D lower than the marginal rate of tax

11 The Laffer curve shows the relationship between the rate of tax and the: (AO1) — 1 mark

   A level of real output in an economy

   B revenue that is obtained from the tax

   C size of a budget deficit

   D size of a budget surplus

12 An automatic stabiliser works to: (AO1) — 1 mark

   A ensure that there is a balanced budget

   B guarantee full employment in an economy

   C reduce fluctuations in income over the course of the trade cycle

   D reduce the size of the national debt

13 The liquidity trap is where: (AO1) — 1 mark

   A a financial institution becomes insolvent and goes out of existence

   B an increase in the money supply does not affect the interest rate

   C the interest rate falls when there is an increase in the money supply

   D there is sufficient liquidity in the financial system

Topic 4

The global context

Globalisation

It is important to understand what is meant by globalisation, the different characteristics of globalisation, the causes of globalisation and the impact of globalisation on developed, emerging and developing economies.

The International Monetary Fund has identified four essential features of the concept of globalisation:
- trade and transactions
- capital and investment movements
- migration of people across national boundaries
- the dissemination of knowledge

Globalisation stresses the interdependence of economic, social and cultural activities. The emphasis is on the connectedness of the world's economies. International economic and business activities are now much more common than in the past and there has been an increase in the number of multinational companies operating in the world. Globalisation stresses that economics does not recognise national boundaries and that competition is crucial to the achievement of the maximum level of efficiency in economic activity throughout the world.

1 Explain the characteristics of globalisation. (AO2) — 4 marks

2 Explain the causes of globalisation. (AO2) — 4 marks

Multinational firms

A multinational firm is one which operates in more than one country. This has to involve some form of economic activity in another country. It therefore means more than just selling in different countries. Car companies, for example, often have factories in different countries. A multinational firm that builds a factory in another country is involved in what is termed 'foreign direct investment'.

> **3** Describe what is meant by a multinational firm. (AO1) `2 marks`

International trade

The Heckscher–Ohlin theory

This theory helps to explain why countries trade goods and services with each other. One condition for trade between two countries is that the countries differ in terms of the availability of factors of production, e.g. one country may have a great deal of capital but relatively few workers, while another country may have many workers but relatively few machines. According to the Heckscher–Ohlin theory, a country will specialise in the production of goods and services that it is most suited to produce, i.e. a country will export those goods that are intensive in the use of their more plentiful factor of production, and import those goods that are intensive in the use of their scarce factor. The effect of this is that relative prices, and relative factor prices, in different countries tend to be equated.

> **4** Explain what is meant by the Heckscher–Ohlin theory. (AO2) `4 marks`

Exchange rates

Bilateral, effective, nominal and real exchange rates

A bilateral exchange rate involves a pair of currencies, i.e. it is the rate at which one currency can be exchanged for another.

Effective exchange rates refer to a weighted average of a basket of currencies. The weightings are in relation to the amount of trade involving the different countries.

Nominal exchange rates refer to the value of a currency compared with other currencies without taking into account the inflation rates in the different countries, i.e. they do not show the purchasing power of one currency compared with another.

Real exchange rates refer to the value of a currency compared with other currencies after taking into account the inflation rate in different countries, i.e. they do show the purchasing power of one currency compared to another.

5 What is meant by an 'exchange rate'? (AO1) — 2 marks

6 Explain different measures of exchange rates. (AO2) — 4 marks

Purchasing power parity (PPP) theory

Purchasing power parity refers to the attempt to compare standards of living in different countries by taking into account the price levels in the different countries. Exchange rates are adjusted in order to give comparisons which take into account purchasing power in different countries. The idea is that an amount of money in one currency can be exchanged for an amount of money in another currency, but both will be able to purchase the same basket of products.

The human development index, for example, takes into account comparative living standards through figures for gross national income (GNI) per capita that have been adjusted to take account of PPP. This recognises that without such an adjustment, it will not be possible to make effective comparisons between standards of living in different countries, given that price levels may well vary a great deal between countries.

7 Describe purchasing power parity theory. (AO1) — 2 marks

Trade policies and negotiations

Different methods of protectionism

Protectionism refers to those methods or policies that protect domestic producers in a country from international competition. They are therefore restrictions on international trade.

There are a number of different methods of protectionism that can be used. These include the following:
- tariffs or import duties
- quotas
- subsidies
- exchange controls
- embargoes
- administrative procedures and restrictions
- voluntary export restraints

> **8** Explain the different methods of protectionism. (AO2) *4 marks*

Free trade and protectionism

Free trade refers to trade between countries that is not restricted by any form of import control. This is linked to the theory of comparative advantage and the idea that without any trade barriers, output can be increased where each country specialises in the production of products with the lowest opportunity cost.

The World Trade Organization, established in 1995, replaced the General Agreement on Tariffs and Trade (GATT), which had been established in 1948. The WTO aims to encourage free trade throughout the world. One of its objectives is to encourage trade liberalisation through the reduction of as many trade barriers as possible. It consists of 161 countries.

It attempts to bring down trade barriers through a number of discussions with member countries and these discussions form part of a round of talks. One of the earliest of these was the Uruguay Round and more recently there has been a Doha Round, which started in 2001.

However, not all countries have been in favour of such trade liberalisation, and some of them have used a variety of different methods to protect domestic producers from international competition. This approach is known as protectionism.

The WTO is generally opposed to such an approach, although in certain circumstances protectionism has been supported — for example, in the case of dumping, where imports into a country are not only cheap, but actually below the cost of production in the country where they were made. This is widely seen not as a positive result of the application of the theory of comparative advantage, but as an unfair practice.

9 Analyse why some countries may prefer protectionism to free trade. (AO3) **12 marks**

10 Evaluate the role of the World Trade Organization in promoting free trade. (AO4) **12 marks**

The stages of economic integration

There are various stages in the process of economic integration, and these can include the following:

- free-trade areas
- customs unions
- single markets
- economic unions
- monetary unions

11 Explain the different stages of economic integration. (AO2) — *4 marks*

Examples of economic integration

There are many examples of economic integration in the world today. These include the European Union, the North American Free Trade Agreement and the Association of South East Asian Nations.

EU (European Union)

The EU can trace its origins to the creation of the European Economic Community in 1958 when it comprised France, Germany, Italy, the Netherlands, Belgium and Luxembourg. The United Kingdom joined in 1973. The EU now consists of 28 countries, 19 of which have adopted a single currency, the euro. The UK is one of nine countries in the EU that has decided to retain its own currency.

In June 2016, the UK held a referendum to decide whether it should remain in, or leave, the EU. The majority decision was to leave the EU. This process is likely to take at least 2 years, and will then leave the EU with 27 members.

NAFTA (North American Free Trade Agreement)

NAFTA consists of three countries: the United States of America, Canada and Mexico. It is a free-trade area, but each of the three countries retains its own barriers on trade with countries outside of the Free Trade Agreement.

ASEAN (Association of South East Asian Nations)

This Association was established in 1967 with five members: Thailand, Indonesia, Malaysia, Singapore and the Philippines. It has gradually grown in size over the years and now consists of ten countries. The five additional countries are Brunei, Cambodia, Laos, Myanmar and Vietnam.

12 Evaluate the advantages and disadvantages of membership of the European Union. (AO4) — *12 marks*

Exam-style questions

13 Look at the following table and then answer the question.

Nominal effective rate of £	82.2
Real effective rate of £	90.1
	2005 = 100

Explain the difference between the nominal and the real effective rate of the pound. (AO2)

6 — 4 marks

14 Evaluate the impact of multinational firms on the world economy. (AO4) [25 marks]

For multiple-choice questions, circle the letter of the answer that you think is correct.

15 A real exchange rate takes into account: (AO1)　　　　　　　　　　　　　　　1 mark

　A　economic growth rates in different countries

　B　inflation rates in different countries

　C　the size of the private sector in different countries

　D　unemployment rates in different countries

16 Which of the following best describes a quota? (AO1)　　　　　　　　　　　　1 mark

　A　A limit on the amount of a good which can be imported

　B　A payment to a firm to keep down its costs of production

　C　A restriction on foreign currency used to buy imports

　D　A tax on the imports of goods into a country

17 Which of the following countries does not use the euro? (AO1)　　　　　　1 mark

　A　Denmark

　B　Latvia

　C　Lithuania

　D　Spain

Topic 5

The financial sector

The role of the financial sector in the real economy

The functions of money

Money has four functions in an economy:
- a medium of exchange
- a unit of account or measure of value
- a store of value or of wealth
- a standard for deferred payments

1 Explain the functions of money. (AO2) *4 marks*

The characteristics of money

Money has a number of characteristics, including the following:
- acceptability
- portability
- scarcity
- recognisability
- stability of value
- divisibility
- durability
- stability of supply
- uniformity

2 Explain the characteristics of money. (AO2) *4 marks*

Narrow and broad money

It is possible to distinguish between two types of money supply in terms of liquidity: narrow money and broad money.

Narrow money refers to cash in the form of notes and coins or to financial assets that can be turned into cash relatively easily and quickly.

Broad money refers to financial assets that are less liquid and which would take longer to be turned into cash. It includes a variety of deposits that are held in financial institutions.

3 Distinguish between narrow and broad money. (AO1) — 2 marks

Credit creation

Credit creation refers to the process of financial institutions increasing their lending by a multiple of new deposits received. This multiple is known as the credit creation multiplier. A financial institution can keep a relatively small percentage of assets in a relatively liquid form and use the remainder to make loans.

Interest rate determination

There are two theories that can be used to explain how the interest rate in an economy is determined.

One of these is the liquidity preference theory. This is where the demand for money is made up of three different motives for money: the transactions demand for money, the precautionary demand for money and the speculative demand for money. The first two motives are interest inelastic and are known as active balances. The speculative motive is interest elastic and is known as an idle balance. The three motives together create the overall demand for money. The interest rate is determined by the demand for money and the money supply (Figure 11).

The other theory of interest rate determination is the loanable funds theory. This states that the rate of interest is determined by the demand for, and the supply of, loanable funds in financial markets. The rate of interest is therefore a price and is determined, just like any other price in a market, by the interaction of demand and supply (Figure 12). The demand for loanable funds comes from firms wanting to invest, households wanting to buy consumer products and a government aiming to fund a budget deficit. The supply of loanable funds comes from savings.

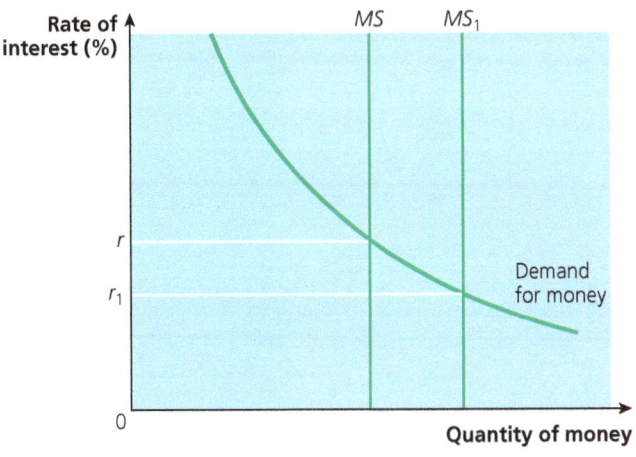

Figure 11 The liquidity preference theory of interest rate determination

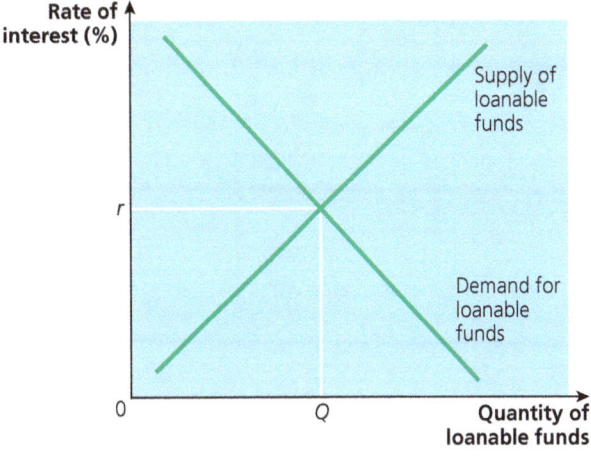

Figure 12 The loanable funds theory of interest rate determination

4. Analyse, with the aid of a diagram, how the interest rate is determined through the liquidity preference theory. (AO3) **8 marks**

5. Analyse, with the aid of a diagram, how the interest rate is determined through the loanable funds theory. (AO3) **8 marks**

The quantity theory of money

The quantity theory of money shows the relationship between the money supply and the price level in an economy. It can be shown through the Fisher equation of exchange, $MV = PT$ (this is sometimes written as $MV = PY$), where M refers to the quantity of money or money supply, V refers to the velocity of circulation of money, P refers to the general level of prices in an economy and T refers to the number of transactions financed by this money. V and T are assumed to be constant, so the theory shows that there is a direct relationship between changes in M and changes in P.

The financial sector in developing and emerging economies

The Harrod–Domar model

The Harrod–Domar model is a theory of economic growth which stresses the importance of the generation of savings which can be used to finance investment. This will increase the productive capacity of an economy and so promote economic development. The theory assumes a constant capital–output ratio. The model therefore shows how much capital investment would be required to bring about a certain level of economic growth, assuming a constant capital–output ratio, and the level of saving that would be required to finance this investment. The model was originally used in relation to developed countries, but it has also been used in relation to developing and emerging economies.

6 Explain the Harrod–Domar model of the promotion of economic development. (AO2) — 4 marks

Microfinance

Microfinance is a broad term which refers to a number of different financial services. Essentially it refers to a source of financial services for borrowers who lack access to mainstream banking and financial services. It is therefore seen as a way of helping poor people escape from poverty and is an example of financial inclusion.

It can also be used by entrepreneurs and small businesses to fund economic activities and so can be seen as a way of promoting economic development, employment and economic growth, especially in developing and emerging economies.

7 Explain what is meant by microfinance. (AO2) — 4 marks

The role of the central bank

The functions of a central bank

A central bank will perform a number of functions in an economy, including the following:
- supporting financial institutions, e.g. by acting as a lender of last resort
- managing the national debt
- acting as banker to the government
- controlling the country's currency through issuing notes and coins
- operating monetary policy, e.g. setting the interest rate
- overseeing the financial system as a whole

8 Explain the functions of a central bank. (AO2) — 4 marks

The independence of the central bank

The Bank of England was granted operational independence by the government in May 1997. In particular, it is allowed to set the interest rate. This decision is taken each month by the Monetary Policy Committee of the Bank of England.

The government, however, retains the power to set the inflation target within which the Bank must operate when carrying out monetary policy. The inflation target is 2% and the governor of the Bank of England must write an open letter to the chancellor of the exchequer if the inflation rate is more than 1% outside of this inflation target.

9 Describe what is meant by the 'independence' of a central bank. (AO1) *2 marks*

Financial regulation

There are three financial regulatory bodies in the UK. These bodies became fully operational in April 2013 when the Financial Services Act 2012 came into effect. The three bodies operate independently and have different objectives, but they do maintain close links with each other in providing an effective system of financial regulation.

The Financial Policy Committee of the Bank of England (FPC)

The FPC is responsible for the survival and stability of the UK financial system. Its main objective is 'identifying, monitoring and taking action to remove or reduce systemic risks with a view to protecting and enhancing the resilience of the UK financial system'.

10 Describe the role of the Financial Policy Committee of the Bank of England (FPC) in financial regulation. (AO1) *2 marks*

The Prudential Regulation Authority (PRA)

The PRA is also part of the Bank of England. It is responsible for the regulation and supervision of over 1,000 financial services providers in the UK, including banks, building societies, credit unions, friendly societies, insurers and investment firms. Its main objective is 'to promote the safety and soundness of financial services providers by requiring them to behave prudently, to minimise the impact on financial stability should a provider fail, and to ensure that financial services continue to be supplied to customers'.

11 Describe the role of the Prudential Regulation Authority (PRA) in financial regulation. (AO1) *2 marks*

The Financial Conduct Authority (FCA)

Unlike the other two institutions, the FCA is separate from the Bank of England. Its main objective is to ensure that the financial markets work well, so that consumers get a fair deal. It has three statutory objectives: to secure an appropriate degree of protection for consumers, to protect and enhance the integrity of the UK financial system and to promote effective competition in the interests of consumers.

12 Describe the role of the Financial Conduct Authority (FCA) in financial regulation. (AO1) — 2 marks

Exam-style questions

13 Explain the credit creation process. (AO2) — 4 marks

14 Explain what is meant by the Fisher equation of exchange. (AO2) — 4 marks

15 Explain how financial institutions are regulated in the UK. (AO2) *(6)* **4 marks**

....
....
....
....
....
....
....
....
....
....

For multiple-choice questions, circle the letter of the answer that you think is correct.

16 Which of the following is a function of money? (AO1) **1 mark**

　A　Ease of recognisability

　B　Medium of exchange

　C　Stability of value

　D　Stability of supply

17 Which of the following is the most liquid? (AO1) **1 mark**

　A　Money deposited in a 7-day account

　B　Money deposited in a 30-day account

　C　Money held in a 1-year bond

　D　Notes in a purse or wallet

18 Which of the following is an example of an 'idle balance'? (AO1) **1 mark**

　A　Emergency demand for money

　B　Precautionary demand for money

　C　Speculative demand for money

　D　Transactions demand for money

19 The Fisher quantity theory of money equation is expressed as: (AO1) **1 mark**

　A　$MP = VT$

　B　$MS = PT$

　C　$MT = PV$

　D　$MV = PT$

Also available

...and many more

Go to http://www.hoddereducation.co.uk/studentworkbooks for details of all our student workbooks.

Hodder Education, an Hachette UK company, Carmelite House, 50 Victoria Embankment, London, EC4 Y0D

Orders
Please contact Hachette UK Distribution, Hely Hutchinson Centre, Milton Road, Didcot, Oxfordshire, OX11 7HH.
tel: 01235 827827
e-mail: education@hachette.co.uk
Lines are open 9.00 a.m.–5.00 p.m., Monday to Friday.
You can also order through the Hodder Education website: www.hoddereducation.co.uk

© Terry Cook 2016
ISBN 978-1-4718-4737-0
First printed 2016
Impression number 5 4
Year 2022

All rights reserved; no part of this publication may be reproduced, stored in a retrieval system, or transmitted, in any form or by any means, electronic, mechanical, photocopying, recording or otherwise without either the prior written permission of Hodder Education or a licence permitting restricted copying in the United Kingdom issued by the Copyright Licensing Agency Ltd, www.cla.co.uk.

Printed in UK

Hachette UK's policy is to use papers that are natural, renewable and recyclable products and made from wood grown in well-managed forests and other controlled sources. The logging and manufacturing processes are expected to conform to the environmental regulations of the country of origin.

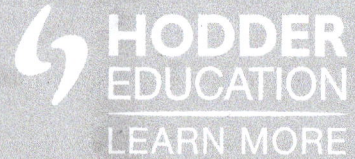